BIOGRAPHY FROM
ANCIENT CIVILIZATIONS
LEGENDS, FOLKLORE, AND STORIES OF ANCIENT WORLDS

The Life and Times of

MOSES

Mitchell Lane
PUBLISHERS

P.O. Box 196
Hockessin, Delaware 19707

BIOGRAPHY FROM

ANCIENT CIVILIZATIONS

LEGENDS, FOLKLORE, AND STORIES OF ANCIENT WORLDS

The Life and Times of

MOSES

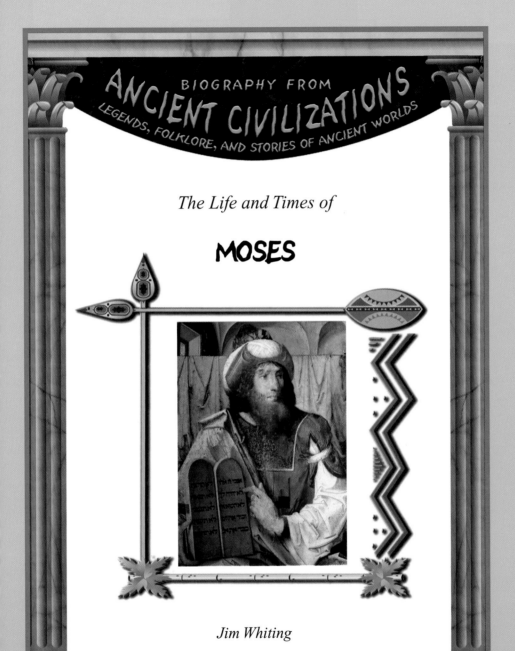

Jim Whiting

Mitchell Lane
PUBLISHERS

Printing   1   2   3   4   5   6   7   8

Library of Congress Cataloging-in-Publication Data

Whiting, Jim, 1943-
    The life and times of Moses / by Jim Whiting.
        p. cm. — (Biography from ancient civilizations)
    Includes bibliographical references (p.) and index.
    ISBN 1-58415-340-7 (library bound)
    1. Moses (Biblical leader)—Juvenile literature. I. Title. II. Series.
    BS580.M6W485 2005

    222'.1092—dc22   2004024602

ABOUT THE AUTHOR: Jim Whiting has been a journalist, writer, editor, and photographer for more than 20 years. In addition to a lengthy stint as publisher of *Northwest Runner* magazine, Mr. Whiting has contributed articles to the *Seattle Times, Conde Nast Traveler, Newsday,* and *Saturday Evening Post.* He has written and edited more than 100 Mitchell Lane titles. He lives in Washington state with his wife and two teenage sons.

PHOTO CREDITS: Cover, pp. 1, 3—Corbis; p. 6—Jamie Kondrchek; p. 9—Hulton/Archive; p. 12—Andrea Pickens; p. 18—Getty Images; pp. 24, 26, 32, 36, 37—Corbis

PUBLISHER'S NOTE: This story is based on the author's extensive research, which he believes to be accurate. Documentation of such research is contained on page 44. However, this story contains speculation and references to people and events that may or may not have existed. The story of Moses might be interpreted differently by some. It is not the author nor the publisher's intent to define history or to declare a set of beliefs more accurate than another. The author has tried to remain neutral by examining all feasible explanations of documented Biblical events so as to give the reader the means to draw his/her own conclusion.

The internet sites referenced herein were active as of the publication date. Due to the fleeting nature of some web sites, we cannot guarantee they will all be active when you are reading this book.

The Life and Times of

Moses

*For Your Information

This is a reproduction of the Ark of the Covenant, which was constructed to hold the tablets containing the Ten Commandments. The Ark disappeared more than 2,500 years ago. Its supposed recovery was the basis for the movie, "Raiders of the Lost Ark."

CHAPTER ONE

MOSES AND THE MOVIES

It is one of the most famous scenes in movie history. At the beginning of the 1981 movie *Raiders of the Lost Ark*, explorer Indiana Jones has just penetrated deep within a mysterious cave. He has dodged several booby traps that have claimed the lives of less experienced men. Gingerly, he lifts a small statue from the pedestal on which it rests. Suddenly he hears an ominous rumbling. To his horror, a huge round boulder begins rolling toward him. He turns and begins running frantically down the passage. The boulder is faster. It grows steadily closer and closer. Ahead of him, the door at the entrance to the cave begins to descend. Diving desperately, Indy rolls under the door—a split second later, he would have been crushed.

The "lost ark" of the title was one of the holiest items in the Jewish religion. Built more than 3,000 years ago and plated with pure gold, the Ark of the Covenant held the Jews' most sacred object: the stone tablets on which the Ten Commandments were inscribed. According to the Bible, they were given directly by God to their leader Moses at the top of Mount Sinai.

For the Jews, the Ark was imbued with God's power. It led them through the desert, destroying snakes, scorpions, and other dangers. It caused the walls of Jericho to fall down. When the Ark was captured by the Philistines, one of their rival groups, it brought down so many plagues and other calamities that it was quickly returned.

For those looking for a more scientific answer to the Ark's powers, there are hints that the Ark may have been history's first electrical harness. "The accounts given of peoples' sudden deaths from touching the Ark are consistent with death by a high voltage, lethal electrical charge," comments David Shyovitz, who writes for the American-Israeli Cooperative Enterprise. "Such a charge could have resulted from the constant exposure of the box to static electricity, which builds up quickly in a hot, dry climate like the Middle East. The materials that the Ark was made of further support this theory: gold is one of the most powerful electrical conductors, and wood is an excellent insulator."[1]

For several centuries, the Ark lay in the innermost sanctuary of the Jewish Temple in Jerusalem. When the Babylonians under King Nebuchadnezzar captured the city in 586 B.C. and carried the Jews into captivity, the Ark disappeared. Its whereabouts remain a mystery to this day.

The plot of *Raiders of the Lost Ark* revolves around the belief that the Ark contains almost unimaginable power. In the movie, German dictator Adolf Hitler wants to locate the Ark and use that power for his own evil ends. (In real life, there is no evidence that Hitler felt this way, although he did commit other horrible crimes against the Jewish people. During World War II, more than 6 million Jews were murdered at his orders.) Despite Indy's best efforts, a group of Hitler's followers capture the Ark. When they open it, its power is unleashed, and all of them are destroyed.

While Moses is not a character in *Raiders of the Lost Ark*, he has been portrayed in several other major Hollywood movies. Famed director Cecil B. De Mille ended his illustrious career with the 1956 film *The Ten Commandments*. It was an audience favorite. Starring Charlton Heston as Moses and Yul Brynner as Rameses the Great—the Egyptian pharaoh, or king, who was his rival—the film depicts the life of Moses from his infancy through his leading the Jewish people out of Egyptian captivity and receiving the Ten Commandments. The image of Moses that this movie presented became very influential. "'I want to see Moses,' one

Dr. Martin Luther King Jr. was an eloquent voice for equal rights for all people. He was awarded the Nobel Peace Prize in 1964. He often echoed Moses' cry to the Pharaoh, "Let my people go!"

delegate to the 1996 Republican National Convention told a newspaper reporter to explain why she was attending a cocktail party featuring Heston."[2]

In 1998, DreamWorks Studios—the same studio that produced such films as *Shrek, Shrek II*, and *Antz*—told the story of Moses in the animated feature *The Prince of Egypt*. Moses and Rameses are shown as being about the same age. The two of them grow up as fast friends—even racing their chariots against each other—before events split them apart. The all-star cast features Val Kilmer as Moses and Ralph Fiennes as Rameses, and also includes Patrick Stewart, Sandra Bullock, Steve Martin, Michelle Pfeiffer, Martin Short, and Danny Glover. Mariah Carey and Whitney Houston sing "The Prince of Egypt (When You Believe)," which won an Academy Award for Best Song.

Moses also has a strong influence today in the real world. Several times in the Bible, God orders Moses to tell the pharaoh, "Let my people go!" Famed civil rights leader Martin Luther King Jr. won the Nobel Peace Prize in 1964. During a lecture at the awards ceremony, he looked back to those moments. "The Bible tells the thrilling story of how Moses stood in Pharaoh's court centuries ago and cried, 'Let my people go,'" Dr. King said. "This is a kind of opening chapter in a continuing story."[3]

Rabbi Levi Meier finds a useful contemporary personal meaning in Moses' story. While considering him "the greatest leader of humanity," Meier adds, "Moses' life, like ours, was not easy. He experienced pain, difficulties, and failures. . . . Moses told his people that if they listened carefully and did what he taught them, they would understand the meaning of life. The words that Moses recorded continue to help each of us find purpose and direction today."[4]

And Jonathan Kirsch points out that Moses is not presented in heroic, larger-than-life terms: "The essential impression of Moses that we are given in the Bible . . . is that he was born like every other infant, grew to manhood with all the impulses and excesses of which real men and women are capable, lived a life marked with passions that are perfectly human, and came to a tragic end."[5]

King Nebuchadnezzar

During the forty-three-year reign of King Nebuchadnezzar, the power and prestige of the empire of Babylon (modern Iraq) reached its peak. He embarked on several successful military campaigns. One of these included the siege and destruction of the Jewish capital of Jerusalem in 586 B.C. He destroyed the temple that had been built by King Solomon about 400 years earlier and took most of the Jewish population to Babylon, keeping them in captivity. While some Jews prospered in Babylon, many endured harsh conditions before they were able to leave fifty years later.

King Nebuchadnezzar

He is also remembered for his construction projects. The most famous is the Hanging Gardens of Babylon, one of the Seven Wonders of the Ancient World. Built on several terraces, it was supposed to remind his wife of the mountainous landscape where she grew up. He also encircled the city with a double wall that measured ten miles around, rebuilt the palace, and oversaw an extensive irrigation system that conveyed water from the Euphrates and Tigris Rivers to countless farms.

According to the biblical book of Daniel, Nebuchadnezzar built a huge statue of himself and ordered three Jewish men who were working for him as administrators—Shadrach, Meshach, and Abednego—to worship it. When they refused to worship anything but God, he ordered them to be thrown into a hot furnace. Protected by God, they emerged unharmed. Nebuchadnezzar was so impressed that he promoted the three men.

The king's vanity and pride soon led to madness. He was afflicted with what is known as lycanthropy (literally, "wolf-person"), in which the sufferer imagines himself as a beast. It lasted for four years, a period during which he was exiled from his throne and was reduced literally to eating grass. He did recover, resumed his throne, and apparently died peacefully of old age.

Because of the associations of the name of Nebuchadnezzar with his country's past glories, former Iraqi dictator Saddam Hussein named one of his army's best units the Nebuchadnezzar Division.

Black Sea

Mediterranean Sea

EGYPT

CANAAN

SINAI PENINSULA

Red Sea

Nile River

Tigris River

MESOPOTAMIA

Euphrates River

ARABIAN DESERT

0   250 miles
    250 kilometers

This map shows where the major events in Moses' life took place. He was probably born just north of the fork in the Nile River. The Sinai Peninsula was his likely destination when he led the Jewish people out of their captivity in Egypt. Canaan is the Promised Land which was his goal.

CHAPTER
TWO

MOSES IN THE BULRUSHES

The only original source we have for the story of Moses is the Bible. His story begins several centuries before the events depicted during his "Hollywood moments." The first major figure is Abraham, a name that means "the father of multitudes." Descended from Noah, Abraham was probably a shepherd in Mesopotamia, or modern Iraq, perhaps as early as 1900 B.C. No one knows for certain because the Bible does not include any specific dates. Nothing is known of his early years, though apparently at a young age he became convinced that there was only a single God, rather than the many gods that his contemporaries worshiped. One day God spoke to Abraham, saying, "Leave your country, your people and your father's household and go to the land I will show you. I will make you into a great nation and I will bless you." (Genesis 12:1-2)[1]

Abraham had no doubts about what he heard. He left his native land and set out with his wife, Sarah; his nephew, Lot; and his servants. After lengthy travels, they arrived in Canaan—the land that he believed he had been promised by God—which is modern Israel and Palestine. After living in Canaan for some years, there was a severe famine. Abraham and his followers went to Egypt, but when conditions eventually improved, they were able to return. Then Abraham's only son, Isaac, was born— even though Abraham was very old and Sarah was long past the normal childbearing age. Their happiness at finally having a son was cut short when God commanded Abraham to sacrifice Isaac. Despite his bitter disappointment, Abraham trusted God and agreed. Just as he raised his knife to kill Isaac, God provided him with a ram instead. Because Abraham had demonstrated his faith, Isaac was spared.

Isaac later had two sons, Jacob and Esau. Jacob—whose name was later changed to the very symbolic Israel—became the heir and had twelve sons. Of those, Joseph was the next-to-youngest and his father's favorite. The other sons were jealous and planned to kill Joseph. At the last moment, they decided to let him live. They threw him down a well, then sold him to a passing caravan on its way to Egypt. Afterward, they smeared goat's blood on a bright coat that Jacob had given to Joseph. The grieving father believed that his son had been killed by a wild animal.

He hadn't. In Egypt, Joseph was sold as a slave to a man named Potiphar. He quickly proved to be very competent, and Potiphar made him his personal favorite. Eventually, because of his ability to interpret dreams, Joseph went into the service of the pharaoh. He predicted that there would be abundant harvests for seven years, followed by seven years of famine. Pharaoh was able to put aside enough food during the abundant years to feed his people during the lean. Because events happened as Joseph had said they would, the impressed pharaoh made him an important official in the government.

During the famine, Joseph's family came to Egypt to request food. They didn't recognize Joseph. This wasn't surprising, because he would have been dressed like an Egyptian. But Joseph recognized them and soon revealed who he was. In view of what they had done to him many years earlier, they expected the worst. Yet Joseph forgave them. Soon the pharaoh allowed them and their father to settle in the land of Goshen, which scholars believe lies in the eastern part of the Nile Delta, and treated them well. When Jacob died, he received one of the highest honors the ancient Egyptians could convey: his body was turned into a mummy. The same honor was extended to Joseph. Just before his death, Joseph said to his brothers, "I am about to die. But God will surely come to your aid and take you up out of this land to the land promised on oath to Abraham, Isaac and Jacob" (Genesis 50:24).

A long period—perhaps up to several centuries—passed. The handful of Israelites from Joseph's era (during their stay in Egypt, they were also referred to as Hebrews, and to this day their language is referred to as Hebrew) thrived in Goshen and greatly expanded their numbers. For most of this period, they apparently lived in harmony with the pharaohs. Eventually a pharaoh who, as the Bible says, "did not know about Joseph," (Exodus 1:8), came to power. Concerned about the steadily growing numbers of Israelites, he decided to enslave them. The only result of their increasingly hard labor was a corresponding increase in the number of Israelites. His next step was to issue an edict that all newborn Israelite babies were to be taken to the Nile River and drowned.

This edict horrified an Israelite woman named Jochebed. Together with her husband, Amram—who was descended from Levi, one of the twelve sons of Jacob—they already had two children, Aaron and Miriam. Jochebed had just given birth to their third child, a little boy. She concealed the infant as long as she could, but it was hard to control a tiny baby. She knew that his crying would eventually give him away. Yet she could not bear to give him up for slaughter. To try to circumvent the harsh punishment, she waterproofed a small wicker basket, put her infant inside, and then, under the watchful eye of her daughter, set it adrift on the Nile.

Miriam soon ran home, happily. She told her mother that the baby had been saved. The little basket had drifted into a clump of bulrushes, tall plants that lined the banks of the Nile. One of pharaoh's daughters found the infant there. Even though she realized that the baby was an Israelite, the young woman took pity on him and decided to adopt him. Turning to the watching Miriam, she told the little girl to find an Israelite to take care of "her" child during his infancy. Miriam had a perfect candidate: her mother. When the little boy was old enough, he was taken to the pharaoh's palace to be with the princess. She named him Moses, which means "drawn from the water."

Even though he spent nearly his entire life among the Egyptians and lived a life of luxury, Moses remained an Israelite in his heart. He never forgot his heritage. One day the now-grown Moses happened to be watching a group of Israelites working. An Egyptian began beating up one of them. In a fit of fury, Moses murdered the Egyptian. Looking around carefully to see if anyone had observed him, he dragged the body away and buried it.

But his crime had been witnessed. The following day, he tried to break up a fight between two Israelites. When he started criticizing them, one of them mocked him, asking him if he planned on killing him just as he had murdered the Egyptian. It may seem strange that the Israelites weren't grateful to Moses for taking their side. They probably were afraid that the pharaoh would take revenge against them for the killing.

It didn't take long for word of the crime to filter up to the pharaoh. He ordered Moses to be executed. Moses escaped and fled into the desert, probably somewhere in the modern Arabian Peninsula in an area known as Midian. No one knows how long he wandered, alone and isolated. One day he came to a well at the same time as the seven daughters of a man named Jethro. Because the daughters didn't have a man with them, a gang of shepherds began bullying them. Moses came to their rescue, drove away the shepherds, and helped them water their flocks. In gratitude, Jethro gave his daughter Zipporah to Moses as his wife. Moses probably looked forward to a peaceful, quiet life in the desert as a shepherd.

But it was not to be. He was about to take part in the greatest human event in the Old Testament.

The Nile River

The Nile River

The longest river in the world, the Nile was the primary reason for the development and success of the ancient Egyptian civilization. It has two primary branches—the White Nile and the Blue Nile—which rise in central Africa and meet in Sudan, the country to the south of modern Egypt.

With inhospitable deserts on both sides, the Nile was the main means of transportation up and down Egypt during most of its history. Its current easily carried boats downriver. For the return trip, sailors took advantage of the prevailing winds and hoisted sails that would propel them upriver.

Even more important was what the ancient Greek historian Herodotus called the "gift of the Nile." Every year the river would overflow its banks, providing precious water in a land with almost no rainfall, and millions of tons of mineral nutrients for farmers to grow their crops. Nearly everyone in Egypt lived within a few miles of the river, primarily on its eastern bank. Because the sun set over the western bank, that side was associated with death and dying. Egyptians called the fertile land by the river "Black Land" because of the color of the mineral-rich soil. Everything else was "Red Land," the distinctive hue of the surrounding desert.

About 100 miles from its outlet in the Mediterranean Sea, the Nile begins to spread out in what is known as the Nile Delta. In ancient times, the river split into seven different branches. These branches emptied into the sea along an arc of about 150 miles. Since then all but two of those branches have been closed, either intentionally or as the result of natural causes. Cairo and Alexandria, Egypt's two largest cities, are located in the Delta.

In 1970, construction of the Aswan High Dam in southern Egypt was completed. Designed to regulate the flow of the river, it created one of the world's largest manmade lakes. Lake Nasser extends southward for more than 300 miles.

Moses spent many years in the desert after fleeing from Egypt. This illustration shows God appearing to him in the form of a burning bush. He was ordered to return to Egypt and free his people.

CHAPTER
THREE

EXODUS

While Moses was getting used to his new life in the desert, the situation of the Israelites grew worse. The pharaoh who had tried to execute Moses died. A new pharaoh—probably someone Moses knew from the years that he had lived at the palace—assumed the throne. He imposed even harsher terms of bondage on the Israelites. According to the Old Testament, God heard their cries for help and decided to take action.

Appearing to Moses in a burning bush, God told Moses that he had appointed him to lead the Israelites out of bondage. Moses shook his head. He replied that he was not great enough.

God would not take no for an answer. He assured Moses that with his—God's—help, he would become great enough for the task. Moses raised another objection. He was a man with little standing. The Israelites were sure to ask who sent him. What could he possibly say to convince them? God thundered his reply: "I AM WHO I AM!" (Exodus 3:14)

Still, Moses wasn't convinced. God turned to trickery, changing Moses' staff into a snake and back again. Moses put his hand into his cloak. When he withdrew it, it was covered with the sores of leprosy. He put it back inside again and was cured. Then God instructed Moses on how to turn water in the Nile into blood. Moses still objected. "I am slow of speech and tongue," he said. (Exodus 4:10) God got angry, saying that

Moses' brother Aaron, already on his way from Egypt for a reunion, would speak for him if he had to. Finally Moses set off.

Moses may have been reluctant to accept the role that had been thrust upon him. Once he had made up his mind, however, he went straight to the pharaoh and told him to release the Israelites. The pharaoh wasn't impressed. He may even have had trouble keeping a straight face. Who was this little man, coming out of the desert, telling him—the most powerful man in the world and a man considered almost godlike by his people—what to do? He didn't have to think twice before dismissing Moses. For good measure, he ordered the Israelites to gather their own straw for their brick making. That only added to their workload. They complained bitterly to Moses that he had made their lives even more miserable.

Moses wasn't a man to give up easily. He and Aaron returned to the palace. Aaron tossed his staff onto the ground, where it became a snake. The pharaoh had his own magicians do the same thing. Their snakes, however, were quickly eaten by Aaron's. It didn't matter. The answer was still no.

God then sent a series of plagues. The Nile turned to blood. Frogs overran the land, which stank horribly when they died. Biting lice attacked everyone. Still no deal. Six more plagues followed in quick succession—swarms of flies, livestock diseases, painful boils, huge hailstones, crop-devouring locusts, and finally three days of complete darkness as the sun was blotted out.

Finally the last—and most horrendous—plague was about to descend. Moses warned Pharaoh that God would kill every firstborn Egyptian son. Pharaoh still refused. Moses passed a word of warning to the Israelites, who made a mark with lambs' blood on their front doors. That way the so-called "Angel of Death" would know to "pass over" the homes of the Israelites. The next morning they awakened to the sound of wailing. Dead Egyptians dotted the landscape. No Israelites had been harmed. This event is the origin of the Jewish holiday of Passover.

That did it. Pharaoh finally allowed the Israelites to depart. A vast caravan set off to the east, so hurriedly that the bread they were baking for the journey had no time to leaven, or rise. (This is why Passover is celebrated with unleavened bread.) Soon, however, Pharaoh changed his mind. To their horror, the Israelites saw a dust cloud behind them, indicating that Pharaoh's soldiers—led by fast-moving horse-drawn chariots—were rapidly closing in on them. Adding to the sense of panic was that they had nearly reached the sea. They appeared to be trapped. As the chariots became visible, God concealed the Israelites in a cloud of smoke. Moses waved his arm, the waters parted, and the Israelites scurried across the seabed to safety on the other side. The smoke disappeared, the chariots rushed after the fugitives, Moses waved his arm again, and the waters collapsed. All the pursuers drowned—including, perhaps, the pharaoh himself.

Traditionally, the body of water that the Israelites crossed has been identified as the Red Sea, which separates northeastern Africa from the Arabian Peninsula. However, the crossing almost certainly did not take place there. The Red Sea is not only more than a hundred miles wide, but it also lies far to the south of the logical route that the Israelites would have taken to make their escape. Another possibility is the Gulf of Suez, the northern arm of the Red Sea, which is closer to Goshen and narrower than the Red Sea. But even a crossing there would have involved a substantial detour—highly unlikely for a large number of people who were anxious to put as much territory as possible between themselves and the land of their bondage.

Another problem with a crossing of the Red Sea is that some scholars believe it is actually a mistranslation of the original Hebrew wording, which they say is "Reed Sea," or "Sea of Reeds." "Red Sea" first appeared sometime during the third century B.C. in a Greek translation. It continued in the Middle Ages in the Latin Bible, and then passed into English with the King James Bible in 1611.

What is more likely is that the crossing occurred at one of the lakes or marshy areas that existed in ancient times between the Nile Delta and the northern end of the Gulf of Suez. Some of these lakes are relatively shallow and relatively close to the Red Sea. But no one knows for sure. The only certainty is that generations of historians have debated the exact location—and will continue to do so.

Classical scholar David Cahill notes, "We should probably imagine this 'sea' as more a marsh than a large body of water; and when Pharaoh, in a change of heart, charges after [the Israelites] with all his chariots and charioteers, we should probably imagine the miracle that we know is coming on a somewhat less heroic scale than its usual dramatizations would have it. . . . [Moses], the true leader, obeying God's directive, leads the Children of Israel through the 'sea,' probably a marsh at low tide. When Pharaoh and his forces follow, they are beset by the rising tide, their wheels get stuck in the mud, and they find themselves in danger of drowning. It would be remembered most gloriously by later generations as a miraculous victory."[1]

As historian David Daiches observes, "The theme that emerges is clear and strong: an army of Egyptian war chariots was destroyed in or beside a body of water in an unexpected and remarkable way. This much must have a historical base."[2]

Perhaps still disbelieving their good fortune—a band of slaves had overcome the might of the pharaoh—the Israelites halted briefly in their flight to celebrate. Miriam—Moses' sister—led a group of women who sang, danced, and played tambourines.

Cahill explains, "This story of deliverance is the central event of the Hebrew scriptures. In retrospect, we can see that all the wanderings of the forefathers and foremothers and their growing intimacy with God have led up to this moment; and looking down the ages from this shore, we can see that everything that happens subsequently will be referred back to this moment of astonished triumph. . . . In this moment, [Abraham's] descendants received an identity they have maintained to this day and remember this barefoot woman, her dark hair having escaped all confinement, singing and dancing on the far shore with prehistoric exuberance."[3]

All too soon the Israelites would come to believe that Miriam's exuberance might have been premature. They had apparently just exchanged one set of problems for another.

Rameses the Great

There is a great deal of speculation about the identity of the pharaoh during the time of the Exodus. As viewers of *The Ten Commandments* and *The Prince of Egypt* are aware, Hollywood believes that he is Rameses II, or Rameses the Great.

Hollywood isn't alone in this belief. Egyptian scholar Joyce Tyldesley writes, "If the biblical story is to be regarded as a true one, rather than as an inspirational tale, who is the unnamed pharaoh? Most experts would agree that it must be [Rameses], with the Exodus far less dramatic and of far less significance to the Egyptians than the Bible would suggest, occurring some time during the first half of his reign. The Egyptian texts make no mention of a time of plagues and runaway workers, nor indeed of parting waters and drowned soldiers, but we would not expect them to; defeat, however minor, did not feature in Egypt's official history."[4]

Rameses the Great

The Bible offers a clue. "They [the Hebrews] built Pithom and Rameses as store cities for Pharaoh" (Exodus 1:11). Also known as Pi-Ramesses, the latter city underwent a massive expansion soon after Rameses became pharaoh in 1279.

At that time he was probably about twenty-five. He would rule for sixty-seven years, the second-longest reign in more than 3,000 years of recorded ancient Egyptian history. As one historian explains, "He was a great military man, he was a man of peace, he was the greatest builder of ancient Egypt, he had the biggest statue, he was the husband of a well-known lady, he had more children than any king of Egypt, he lived longer than any king of Egypt. Even nowadays he has the best preserved mummy."[5]

He also has one of Egypt's most popular tourist attractions: the temple at Abu Simbel on the Nile River, which he built in honor of himself. Four massive statues of Rameses are in front, eight more support the interior, and the highlight is still another statue of Rameses seated next to Amun, Egypt's most important god.

This painting of Moses shows him holding two stone tablets containing the Ten Commandments. God giving the Ten Commandments to Moses is one of the most famous stories in the Bible. But God didn't stop at ten. He gave Moses more than 600 commandments.

CHAPTER
FOUR

INTO THE WILDERNESS

The most direct route from Egypt to Canaan—the Promised Land—would have been along the well-traveled road that lay along the Mediterranean coast. However, that route contained a number of outposts manned by Egyptian troops. The best way of being left alone would be to go somewhere where no one else wanted to go. According to most theories, after their victory celebration, the Israelites turned south, eventually paralleling the eastern shoreline of the Gulf of Suez.

This route put them in the desert in the Sinai Peninsula, which Thomas Cahill terms "one of our planet's most desolate places. It would be hard to conjure up a landscape more likely to lead to death—a land bereft of all comfort, an earth of so few trees and plants that one may walk for hours without seeing a wisp of green, a place so dry that the uninitiated may die in no time, consumed by what seems like preternatural dehydration."[1]

The King James Version of the Bible makes the same point in one of its most memorable phrases: The Sinai Peninsula is a "great and terrible wilderness." The "terrible" part soon became obvious to the Israelites. In Egypt, they may have been slaves. But at least they were relatively well-fed slaves. Now they were free. *Free to suffer*, some of them muttered.

This is a view of the Sinai desert. It clearly reveals how dry and arid it is. Finding food and water was a constant struggle for the Israelites.

They complained that the drinking water at the first spring they found tasted bitter. Moses solved the problem by throwing a chunk of wood into the pool. Then they complained about the lack of food. In the morning God provided manna from heaven—manna was a sort of bread that would become a dietary staple. In the evening, God provided large flocks of quail.

Then there was a double dose of trouble. First there was no water. Moses struck a stone with his staff and fresh water gushed forth. No sooner had the Israelites' thirst been quenched than a strange tribe—the Amalekites—attacked them. An odd thing happened as Moses watched the seesaw battle from a nearby hilltop. When he held up his hands, the Israelites would gain the advantage. When he dropped them, the Amalekites took control. Things began looking bad when Moses—by then a relatively elderly man—got tired and couldn't hold up his hands any longer. His brother Aaron and another man found a nearby boulder, allowed Moses to sit on it, and stood beside him. Each man held up one of Moses' hands. The Israelites won.

The most celebrated event during the Israelites' long sojourn in the wilderness happened soon afterward, just three months after they entered the desert: Moses received the Ten Commandments on Mount Sinai. It was the same location in which he had seen the burning bush.

"So far, everything God had bestowed on the Israelites had been given freely, but now he wanted something in return: a covenant, a formal contract that obliged the Israelites to obey [God's] as-yet-undisclosed law,"[2] writes Jonathan Kirsch. On the appointed morning, a dense cloud enveloped the summit as thunder and lightning filled the skies.

Moses ascended the mountain, then returned to the anxiously waiting Israelites. Surprisingly, there are different interpretations regarding exactly what Moses returned with to show them. "The text of the Ten Commandments is not exactly the same in every version of the Bible," says Kirsch. "Even the numbering of the Ten Commandments is obscure; Jewish tradition starts counting with the phrase 'I am the Lord thy God,' but Christian tradition regards 'Thou shalt have no other gods before me' as the First Commandment."[3] Some groups consider both of these together as the First Commandment.

According to the New International Version of the Bible, the Ten Commandments read, in part, as follows:

I am the Lord your God.

You shall have no other gods before me.

You shall not make for yourself an idol.

You shall not misuse the name of the Lord your God.

Remember the Sabbath day by keeping it holy.

Honor your father and your mother.

You shall not murder.

You shall not commit adultery.

You shall not steal.

You shall not give false testimony against your neighbor.

You shall not covet your neighbor's house. You shall not covet your neighbor's wife, or his manservant or maidservant, his ox or donkey, or anything that belongs to your neighbor. (Exodus 20:2-17)

Many scholars believe that in the original Hebrew version, each of the Ten Commandments consisted of just a single word, such as "no-kill" or "no-idols." In fact, a term that is often used to refer to the Ten Commandments is Decalogue, which literally means "list of ten words." Such a simple system would make it easy for people with almost no education to keep track of the commandments on their ten fingers.

Regardless of the variations, millions of people are familiar with the basic story of the Ten Commandments. What is not quite so familiar is that God didn't stop at ten. Or twenty. Or thirty. Or even one hundred. God kept going, giving Moses a long list of rules and regulations that finally reached a total of 613.

As author Bruce Feiler writes, "Moses repeats these laws, commonly known as the Book of the Covenant, because it amounts to a contract between God and the people, an expansion of the verbal agreement first reached between God and Abraham. To press the importance of these laws, Moses has the population agree to follow them by sprinkling bull's blood on the people. As he says, 'This is the blood of the covenant which the Lord now makes with you concerning these commands.'"[4]

This was a significant moment in Israelite history. Feiler continues, "Up to now, the Israelites have been largely passive—receiving the protection of God, being freed from slavery—but promising little in return. Now they become active participants in the covenant, agreeing publicly to follow the dictates of God. Mount Sinai marks their birth as a spiritual nation, one committed not merely to conquering and holding power at all costs, but to do so within a strict moral framework."[5]

There was just one hitch in this process. God soon called Moses back up the mountain. He spent forty days there, wrapped in a cocoon of smoke that made him invisible to the Israelites waiting thousands of feet below. He received additional instructions on a number of subjects, such as the method of building the Ark of the Covenant and the way in which

The Israelites grew impatient while Moses was receiving the Ten Commandments. They began worshiping a golden calf. Moses and God were outraged when they saw it and severely punished the Israelites.

priests should dress. When God finished, he gave Moses a pair of stone tablets. Engraved on them were the Ten Commandments.

Unfortunately, the Israelites proved to have little patience during Moses' extended absence. Believing—or perhaps fearing—that Moses had abandoned them, they asked Aaron to provide them with a different god to worship. The accommodating Aaron told them to remove their golden earrings and melt them into the image of a golden calf—a familiar image in Egyptian religion. Back in their comfort zone, the Israelites enjoyed a lavish celebration.

Outraged, God threatened to destroy them. Moses, halfway down, urged restraint. But when he got to the bottom and saw what had been going on, he became just as enraged and smashed the two tablets. He rushed over to the idol, threw it into the fire, ground up what was left, stirred it into water, and ordered the Israelites to drink it. Much worse, he called on his kinsmen—the Levites, who by then had become identified as the class of priests—to attack the crowd. They killed three thousand of their fellows in a short time.

After this bloody purge, Moses addressed the Israelites. He criticized them for sinning, but told them that he thought he could persuade God to forgive them. He went back up the mountain for another forty-day sojourn, during which he received a new set of stone tablets. On the way down, his face became so radiant—giving off beams of light—that no one could look directly on his face. He had to begin wearing a veil, lifting it only when he was in the presence of God. David Daiches writes, "This is a fascinating symbol of the consequences of Moses' increasing communion with the divine: his lonely mystic visions, while not impairing his leadership, were increasingly setting him apart from the people."[6]

Once again, there was a translation error. The Hebrew word for "radiant" was recorded as "horn" during the Middle Ages when the Bible was translated into Latin. When famous Italian painter and sculptor Michelangelo carved a massive marble statue of Moses in the sixteenth century, he included two stubby horns on top of Moses' head. This translation error even led some people to believe that all Jews looked this way. Kirsch writes, "My junior high journalism teacher, a Jewish man who served in World War II, recalled that he woke up one night in the barracks to find a fellow draftee, a man from the rural South, kneeling by his bunk and staring at the top of his head. 'I've never met a Jew before,' the soldier explained, 'and I wanted to see your horns.'"[7]

When they had been given the laws—their assurance that they were the "Chosen People" of God—it was time to move on. The Promised Land lay not far away. The Israelites built a container for the stone tablets on which the commandments were engraved—the Ark of the Covenant—and set out from Mount Sinai. They appeared to be well-organized and well-armed, ready to defeat any force that might oppose them. Hopes were high. They thought their days of hardship in the desert were over.

They thought wrong.

The Rest of the 613 Commandments

The Ten Commandments were just the beginning of the rules that God gave to Moses, who in turn passed them on to the people he was leading. These rules make up one of the most important parts of the Torah, or "Teaching," the name that Jews give to the first five books of the Old Testament.

Probably the most famous of the remaining 603 is the *lex talionis* (law of retaliation), which contains the injunction, "If there is serious injury, you are to take life for life, eye for eye, tooth for tooth, hand for hand, foot for foot, burn for burn, wound for wound, bruise for bruise." (Exodus 21:23-25) To some people, "an eye for an eye" justifies revenge. At the time of Moses, however, as Jonathan Kirsch explains, it was "actually far less harsh in practice than the laws of

The Torah

neighboring civilizations of the ancient Near East because it was not inter-preted literally and meant only that punishment should be in proportion to the wrongdoing that was being punished."[8]

Other commandments became the basis for Jewish kosher, or "clean," dietary practices. An example of these is "Do not cook a young goat in its mother's milk." (Exodus 23:19)

Still others reflect beliefs of the time—such as putting witches to death, burning certain offenders alive, and the proper way to deal with slaves—that have long since become obsolete.

As classical scholar Thomas Cahill notes, "This long-winded, unwieldy compilation of assorted prescriptions represents an overall softening—a humanizing—of the common law of the ancient Middle East, which easily prescribed a hand not for a hand but for the theft of a loaf of bread or for the striking of one's better and which gave much favor to the rights of the nobility and virtually none to the lower classes. . . . Rather, in the prescriptions of Jewish law we cannot but note a presumption that all people, even slaves, are human and that all human lives are sacred."[9]

1377. ROMA - Chiesa di S. Pietro in Vincoli - Mosè di Michelangelo

This statue of Moses was carved by the famous Italian sculptor and painter Michelangelo. It is located at the tomb of Pope Julius II in Rome. The small horns at the top of Moses' head were the result of a mistranslation of the Hebrew words for "radiant light."

CHAPTER
FIVE

TO THE PROMISED LAND

Old habits die hard. Almost as soon as the march began, the Israelites resumed their complaining. This time they were grousing about the food. The constant diet of manna was becoming monotonous. They still had fond memories of full bellies when they lived in Egypt: meat, fish, cucumbers, melons, leeks, onions, and garlic.

Soon they had a lot more to complain about. As they approached the Promised Land, Moses acted prudently. Establishing a base camp at an oasis called Kadesh, he sent out a group of spies to provide firsthand reports of what lay ahead of them. They returned after forty days with good news and bad news. The good news was that the land flowed with milk and honey. And fruit. Staggering under their burdens, some of the men brought in ripe grapes, pomegranates, and figs to reveal the richness of the land.

The bad news was that the people who already inhabited Canaan—Amalekites, Hittites, Jebusites, and Amorites, in addition to the Canaanites themselves—collectively composed a formidable force. Only two of the spies—Joshua (Moses' eventual successor as leader of the Israelites) and Caleb—urged immediate action. The others recited one horror story after another about the strength of their opponents. Some of them were giants. It would be almost hopeless to go any farther.

The Israelites were dismayed. Many cried that they wished they had died in Egypt. Others demanded the right to select new leadership and an immediate return to Egypt.

God, once again angered, threatened to destroy the Israelites. Moses again talked him out of it. Still incensed, God thundered that with the exceptions of Caleb and Joshua, the current generation—people aged twenty and over—would never see the Promised Land because they doubted him. He decreed a proportional punishment: a year in the wilderness for every day the scouts had been gone. That added up to 40 years.

Again there was a rebellion against Moses. Three men claimed that Moses and his brother Aaron had placed themselves too high. Moses proposed a test. Both sides would burn incense, and God would make the decision. Moments later the earth opened up and swallowed the three opponents. At the same time, a fireball destroyed 250 of their supporters who were waiting nearby.

The Israelites were outraged. A mob began to form, threatening to attack Moses and Aaron. God sent a plague, threatening a holocaust that would consume the entire population. The two leaders intervened and the plague ended, but not before 15,000 Israelites died, five times more than had perished during the episode of the golden calf.

This continued a pattern that characterizes much of the story of Moses. According to Bruce Feiler, "God performs miracles—brings water from the well, rains manna from the heavens, delivers the Ten Commandments—and the Israelites react in ungrateful ways. Repeatedly God threatens to kill them and start over with Moses, as he had with Abraham, as he had with Noah. In each case God is mollified, though not before exacting a huge price from the Israelites. . . .

"As is the case in international relations, the only way to stop a downward spiral is with enlightened leadership, and Moses, even in his most trying times, emerges as an enlightened leader. Specifically what Moses realizes is that God and Israel need each other, and that it's his role to make sure that happens, to play peacemaker. Time and again throughout the rebellions, Moses pleads with God to forgive the people, then turns around and pleads with the people not to be so hardheaded toward God."[1]

In other words, Moses was a negotiator, and a very good one at that. He needed to be to keep the people together in their forty years of isolation. But he failed at one crucial moment. It would cost him dearly.

The Bible tells us virtually nothing of what happened during those years in the wilderness. The Israelites may have spent most of the time at Kadesh. Their large numbers threatened to exhaust the fresh water at the oasis. God instructed Moses to speak to a nearby rock, which would then produce sufficient water. Moses walked over to the rock, struck it with his staff—the same method he had used soon after the Israelites had arrived in the desert following their flight from Egypt. That was a mistake. He hadn't precisely followed God's instructions. He had struck the rock, rather than speaking to it. Retribution was immediate. "You will not bring this community into the land I give them," God said. (Numbers 20:12)

The Bible is silent about the way in which Moses received this harsh edict. It must have been crushing to his spirit. "Against the blow of a wooden staff upon a dry rock, a lifetime of struggle, hardship, and faithful service counted for nothing in the eyes of [God]," writes Jonathan Kirsch.[2]

Moses knew that he wouldn't enter the Promised Land, but it was still his duty to lead the Israelites there. When the period of punishment ordained by God was over, it was time to make plans. These plans took advantage of what had happened during the past 40 years. As Feiler explains, "The desert is a cauldron where the Israelites must coalesce. The desert not only cleanses, it constructs. . . . Because the place is demanding, it builds character; because it's destructive, it builds interdependence; because it's isolating, it builds community. Because it's the desert, it builds nations."[3]

The Israelites had truly come together as a people.

The path to the Promised Land was still blocked to approaches from the south. Therefore, Moses decided on an "end-around." In other words,

The Jordan River, pictured here, was important during Biblical times. It marked one boundary of the Promised Land. The river was also the site of Jesus' baptism by John the Baptist.

the Israelites would try to make their entrance from the opposite direction. They set out northward but quickly ran into opposition. The kingdom of Edom refused to let them pass. Moses swung eastward, skirting the Edomites. Then he headed north again. Toughened by their years in the wilderness, the Israelites overcame the Amorites. The kingdom of Moab—the final stop before the Promised Land—lay just ahead. Panic-stricken, the Moabite king asked a sorcerer named Balaam to lay a curse on his new—and unwelcome—neighbors. Instead, inspired by God, Balaam issued a blessing for the intruders, who swept into Moab and made camp near the Jordan River. The Promised Land was on the other side.

It was time for Moses to speak to the people he had led so long and so far for the final time. As Jonathan Kirsch writes, "The saga that began on the banks of the Nile came to an end on the banks of the Jordan. . . . The Israelites were no longer the ragged band of runaway slaves whom Moses had led out of Egypt so many years before. The slave generation was dead and gone, and their children had proved themselves to be a

This stone is on Mount Nebo. It is the site from which Moses was allowed to see the Promised Land before he died. Located in northwest Jordan, the mountain is about 2,500 feet high.

generation of warriors, tough and ruthless. As Moses spoke his last words to the nation of Israel, the disciplined ranks of battle-hardened soldiers gathered before him were ready for the command that would send them across the Jordan River at last."[4]

Moses was not destined to make that crossing. He ascended to the top of Mount Nebo, where God showed him the land that his followers were about to claim. Then he died.

Bruce Feiler writes, "It seems impossibly sad that Moses could lead the Israelites out of Egypt, direct them for forty years in the desert, beat back their many rebellions, only to be stopped just inches from the Promised Land."[5]

But the first five books of the Old Testament—also known as the Torah, the Pentateuch, and the Five Books of Moses—do not end in tragedy. It ends with praise of Moses. "Since then, no prophet has risen in Israel like Moses, whom the Lord knew face to face, who did all those miraculous signs and wonders the Lord sent him to do in Egypt—to Pharaoh and to all his officials and to his whole land. For no one has ever shown the mighty power or performed the awesome deeds that Moses did in the sight of all Israel." (Deuteronomy 34:10-12)

Today, the covenant remains. Though Judaism has less than 14 million adherents around the world—there are an estimated 1.9 billion Christians and more than a billion Muslims—it exerts a force far beyond mere numbers. Judaism led directly to Christianity, and many of its prophets are accepted as important elements of the religion of Islam—including Moses, whose Arabic name is Muse. His name appears 136 times in the Quran, the most of any prophet in the Islamic holy book.

"Moses was without doubt the most powerful genius brought forth by Israel," concludes author Elias Auerbach. "In order to achieve what he did, he possessed a variety of talents, which in their abundance and breadth have rarely been concentrated in a single man. . . . He had to have all the ability of a statesman and army commander; he had to be able to assume the leadership of a people and to deal with the pressing dangers of every hour; he needed infallible judgment and the ability to make prompt decisions. . . . He had to provide food and water. He had to give guidance on the way and provide security.

"He traveled that route with unerring certainty for forty years, day by day and year by year, until his work was crowned with success: such success that the coming generations felt themselves to be the heirs and successors of his course. With all the detail—and in small things lies the truly great!—he remained the prophetic visionary who conceived the final accomplishment and its continuance in a hostile world."[6]

The Bible as History

Outside of the Bible, there is only one contemporary reference to events during and immediately following the time of Moses. A victory monument erected by Merneptah—Rameses' successor as pharaoh—in 1207 B.C. says, "Israel is devastated, her seed is no more."[7] Therefore, since the Bible is virtually our only source of information about Moses, is it accurate?

Some people believe Bible writers wrote exactly what God told them to write. Others believe the writers adapted memories of actual events. For example, the Greek island of Santorini underwent a cataclysmic volcanic eruption around 1650 B.C. Dirt and ash darkened the skies for days—echoed by the ninth plague just before the Exodus. The eruption probably caused a tidal wave that could have lowered and then raised water levels—and have explained how Moses parted the sea.

FYI
For Your Info

Merneptah

However, as history professor Norman Cantor believes, "Abraham, Isaac, Jacob, Moses—if they ever lived, if they were real historical figures, there is no basis for believing so outside the Hebrew Bible itself. . . . What is given in the Bible about Jewish origins are made-up stories created from a much later time."[8]

On the other hand, David Cahill says, "The text of the Bible is full of clues that the authors are attempting to write history of some sort. . . . There is in these tales a kind of specificity—a concreteness of detail, a concern to get things right—that convinces us that the writer has no doubt that each of the main events he chronicles happened."[9]

David Daiches notes, "The biblical account of Moses is not history as we understand it: it represents the coming together of a variety of traditions. . . . Yet the history underlying it is real; Moses was a real person; the exodus from Egypt and the entry into the Promised Land were real events; and the religious experience that the Bible tells us Moses first underwent with his flock of sheep in the wilderness of Midian was a genuine experience undergone by the man who remolded the religious consciousness of his people and in doing so made possible the history of both Judaism and Christianity."[10]

Perhaps it doesn't matter. As Rabbi Arnold Jacob Wolf, a noted Jewish scholar, writes, "It was never the 'historical' Moses who really counted for Judaism. Not who Moses was but what Moses signified and taught was always the crucial issue and it still is."[11]

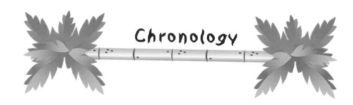

Chronology

Exact dates are unknown

- Born in Egypt
- Is set adrift in the Nile River and discovered by an Egyptian princess
- Raised in the palace of the pharaoh
- Murders an Egyptian
- Under the threat of execution, flees into the desert
- Marries Zipporah
- Meets God in a burning bush and is persuaded to return to Egypt
- Back in Egypt, finally persuades pharaoh to let his people go after a series of ten plagues
- Avoids recapture by pharaoh's soldiers as he and the Israelites escape across the Sea of Reeds (sometimes called the Red Sea)
- Leads Israelites into the desert
- Receives the Ten Commandments
- Shatters stone tablets containing the Ten Commandments when the Israelites worship a golden calf
- Gets second set of stone tablets with the Ten Commandments
- Builds Ark of the Covenant to hold them
- Sets out for Promised Land
- Forced to spend forty years in the wilderness when the Israelites are reluctant to enter the Promised Land
- Leads the Israelites to the Jordan River, across from the Promised Land
- Glimpses the Promised Land from Mount Nebo, then dies

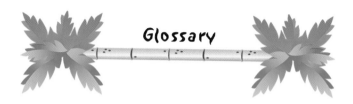

Glossary

boils	(BOYLZ)—painful skin inflammation that includes swelling.
cauldron	(KAWL-drun)—a kettle with boiling water; a situation involving intense emotions.
circumvent	(sur-cum-VENT)—to go around in order to avoid doing something.
coalesce	(koe-uh-LESS)—to come together to form a whole.
covenant	(KUV-nunt)—a formal agreement among two or more parties.
draftee	(draf-TEE)—a person who is forced to do military service.
edict	(EE-dikt)—an order with the force of law.
holocaust	(HAH-luh-kost)—massive destruction that includes extensive loss of life.
mystic	(MIS-tick)—mysterious; producing wonder or awe.
Old Testament	(OLD TES-tuh-ment)—the first part of the Christian Bible, containing the books sacred to Jews.
preternatural	(pree-tur-NA-chuh-ruhl)—going beyond what is natural or ordinary.
purge	(PURJ)—to eliminate members or a group who are regarded as disloyal of threatening.

Timeline
in History

B.C.

3100   Earliest recorded Egyptian history, the Early Dynastic Period, begins.

1304   Rameses the Great is born.

1279   Rameses begins his reign as pharaoh.

1212   Rameses dies; Merneptah succeeds him.

1200   According to legend, the Trojan War begins and lasts for ten years.

1000   David becomes king of the united kingdoms of Judah and Israel and establishes Jerusalem as the capital.

961   Solomon becomes king with the death of his father David; he builds the First Temple; the kingdom of Judah and Israel reaches its greatest extent during his reign.

925   Solomon dies.

776   The first Olympic Games are held in Olympia, a small Greek city-state.

753   Romulus founds the city of Rome.

586   The Babylonians under King Nebuchadnezzar capture Jerusalem and carry off the inhabitants as captives.

539   Jewish exiles return from Babylon.

516   The Second Temple is dedicated in Jerusalem.

Timeline
in History

B.C.

332   Alexander the Great conquers Jerusalem.

63   The Romans capture Jerusalem.

A.D.

66   The Jewish revolt against Roman occupation begins.

70   Roman forces crush the revolt, destroy the Second Temple, and
         force the Jews into exile.

135   Roman emperor Hadrian uses the word Palestine (derived from
         name of the Philistines, one of the Jews' former enemies) to
         refer to the land of Judah and Israel.

640   Jerusalem becomes a holy site for Muslims.

1099   Christian soldiers capture Jerusalem during the First Crusade
         and massacre the defenders.

1187   Muslim leader Saladin recaptures Jerusalem from the
         Crusaders.

1896   Hungarian journalist Theodor Herzl proposes a Jewish state in
         Palestine.

1948   The nation of Israel is established.

2004   A Methodist Church in the United Kingdom holds contest
         asking entrants to name their favorite "Eleventh
         Commandment."

BIOGRAPHY FROM
ANCIENT CIVILIZATIONS
LEGENDS, FOLKLORE, AND STORIES OF ANCIENT WORLDS

For Further
Reading

For Young Adults

McCaughrean, Geraldine. *God's People: Stories from the Old Testament.* New York: Margaret K. McElderry Books, 1997.

Odjik, Pamela. *The Israelites.* Englewood Cliffs, N.J.: Silver Burdett Press, 1989.

Sherman, Josepha. *Your Travel Guide to Ancient Israel.* Minneapolis: Lerner Publications Company, 2004.

Waldman, Neil. *The Golden City: Jerusalem's 3000 Years.* New York: Atheneum Books for Young Readers, 1995.

Works Consulted

The Holy Bible, New International Version. Grand Rapids, Mich.: Zondervan Publishing House, 1994.

Auerbach, Elias. *Moses.* Translated and edited by Robert A. Barclay and Israel O. Lehmann. Detroit: Wayne State University Press, 1975.

Cahill, Thomas. *The Gifts of the Jews.* New York: Doubleday, 1998.

Cantor, Norman. *The Sacred Chain: The History of the Jews.* New York: HarperCollins, 1994.

Clayton, Peter A. *Chronicle of the Pharaohs.* New York: Thames and Hudson, 1994.

Daiches, David. *Moses.* New York: Praeger Publishers, Inc., 1975.

Feiler, Bruce. *Walking the Bible.* New York: HarperCollins, 2001.

Kirsch, Jonathan. *Moses: A Life.* New York: Ballantine Books, 1998.

Meier, Rabbi Levi. *Moses: The Prince, the Prophet.* Woodstock, Vt.: Jewish Lights Publishing, 1998.

For Further
Reading

Tyldesley, Joyce. *Ramesses: Egypt's Greatest Pharaoh.* New York: Viking, 2000.

On the Internet

Cook, Clarence. "Nebuchadnezzar."

http://www.mainlesson.com/display.php?author=horne&book=soldiers&story=
nebuchadnezzar

Spiro, Rabbi Ken. "Crash Course in Jewish History"

http://www.aish.com/literacy/jewishhistory/

King, Dr. Martin Luther. "Dr. Martin Luther King—Nobel Lecture."

http://nobelprize.org/peace/laureates/1964/king-lecture.html

Department of Geography at Oklahoma State University: "Lower Nile River
Valley."

http://www.geog.okstate.edu/1113web/thelower.htm

GlobalSecurity.org: "Nebuchadnezzar Division."

http://www.globalsecurity.org/military/world/iraq/nebuchadnezzar.htm

Shyovitz, David. "The Lost Ark of the Covenant."

http://www.jewishvirtuallibrary.org/jsource/Judaism/ark.html

The Learning Channel: "Moses and the Exodus"

http://tlc.discovery.com/convergence/moses/moses.html

Wolf, Arnold Jacob. "Moses at the Millenium."

http://www.findarticles.com/p/articles/mi_m0411/is_1_49/ai_61887414

Chapter Notes

CHAPTER ONE   *MOSES AND THE MOVIES*

1. David Shyovitz, "The Lost Ark of the Covenant," http://www.jewishvirtuallibrary.org/jsource/Judaism/ark.html

2. Jonathan Kirsch, *Moses: A Life* (New York: Ballantine Books, 1998), p. 6.

3. Dr. Martin Luther King, "Dr. Martin Luther King—Nobel Lecture," http://nobelprize.org/peace/laureates/1964/king-lecture.html

4. Rabbi Levi Meier, *Moses: The Prince, the Prophet* (Woodstock, Vermont: Jewish Lights Publishing, 1998), pp. 2–3.

5. Kirsch, p. 1.

CHAPTER TWO   *MOSES IN THE BULRUSHES*

1. All Bible verses quoted in text are from The Holy Bible, New International Version (Grand Rapids, Mich.: Zondervan Publishing House, 1994).

CHAPTER THREE   *EXODUS*

1. Thomas Cahill, *The Gifts of the Jews* (New York: Doubleday, 1998), pp. 118–19.

2. David Daiches, *Moses* (New York: Praeger Publishers, Inc., 1975), p. 93.

3. Cahill, pp. 121–22.

4. Joyce Tyldesley, *Ramesses: Egypt's Greatest Pharaoh* (New York: Viking, 2000), p. 57.

5. Bruce Feiler, *Walking the Bible* (New York: HarperCollins, 2001), p. 175.

CHAPTER FOUR   *INTO THE WILDERNESS*

1. Thomas Cahill, *The Gifts of the Jews* (New York: Doubleday, 1998), pp. 132–33.

2. Jonathan Kirsch, *Moses: A Life* (New York: Ballantine Books, 1998), p. 242.

3. Ibid., p. 248.

Chapter Notes

4. Bruce Feiler, *Walking the Bible* (New York: HarperCollins, 2001), p. 258.

5. Ibid.

6. David Daiches, *Moses* (New York: Praeger Publishers, Inc., 1975), p. 140.

7. Kirsch, p. 5.

8. Ibid., p. 252.

9. Cahill, p. 154.

CHAPTER FIVE   TO THE PROMISED LAND

1. Bruce Feiler, *Walking the Bible* (New York: HarperCollins, 2001), pp. 324–25.

2. Jonathan Kirsch, *Moses: A Life* (New York: Ballantine Books, 1998), pp. 306–07.

3. Feiler, pp. 347–48.

4. Kirsch, pp. 328–30.

5. Feiler, p. 427.

6. Elias Auerbach, *Moses*, translated and edited by Robert A. Barclay and Israel O. Lehmann (Detroit: Wayne State University Press, 1975), pp. 215–16.

7. Peter A. Clayton, *Chronicle of the Pharaohs* (New York: Thames and Hudson, 1994), p. 157.

8. Norman Cantor, *The Sacred Chain: The History of the Jews* (New York: HarperCollins, 1994), p. 3.

9. Thomas Cahill, *The Gifts of the Jews* (New York: Doubleday, 1998), pp. 126–27.

10. David Daiches, *Moses* (New York: Praeger Publishers, Inc., 1975), pp. 9–10.

11. Arnold Jacob Wolf, "Moses at the Millenium."

http://www.findarticles.com/p/articles/mi_m0411/is_1_49/ai_61887414

Index